The BACHELOR
— BINGO GAME BOOK —

By Jenine Zimmers
Copyright © 2023

Welcome, Bachelor Nation fans!

The Bachelor Bingo Game works similarly to a traditional bingo game. Each square has a Bachelor-themed event or saying. As you watch the show and the drama unfolds, mark off the squares that you see or hear. (Bingo tip: Read through your card beforehand so you'll know what to look for.) To win the game, complete a full row – either horizontal, vertical or diagonal!

You can play alone or with others at a Bachelor viewing party. Simply cut out the bingo cards from the book that you would like to use. There are 8 bingo cards for each of the following:

1. Any regular season episode of "The Bachelor"
2. "The Bachelor" premier episode
3. The hometown dates episode
4. The fantasy suites episode
5. The finale of "The Bachelor"
6. Any regular season episode of "Bachelor in Paradise"

Want to reuse your bingo cards? Use pennies to mark off your squares instead of pen or pencil.

Optional game challenge: You can play until the end of the episode, and whoever marks off the most squares wins!

In the back of the book are two bonus games: The Limo Arrival Card Game, and The Bachelor Nation Villains Trivia Game. To play, cut out the cards, and place them face down in a stack. Take turns reading and answering questions. One point is awarded for each card. The person who has the most points at the end wins! You may play each game separately, or combine them into one card game.

Thanks for playing, and enjoy!

Bingo for the right reasons!

The
BACHELOR
Bingo

SOMEONE SAYS THE WORD "JOURNEY"	SOMEONE SHARES A PERSONAL SOB STORY	SOMEONE KISSES THE BACHELOR IN FRONT OF OTHERS	SOMEONE JUMPS INTO THE BACHELOR'S ARMS	SOMEONE SIPS THEIR DRINK
SOMEONE HAS TOO MUCH TO DRINK	THE POOL IS SHOWN	HOST: "THIS IS THE FINAL ROSE TONIGHT"	THE HOST FIRST APPEARS	A LIMO ARRIVES
YOU SEE A GLASS OF WHITE WINE	THE BACHELOR ENTERS THE ROOM	This free space isn't here to make friends.	SOMEONE IS WEARING A NECKLACE	SOMEONE WEARS A SILLY COSTUME
SOMEONE GIVES THE BACHELOR A GIFT	SOMEONE SAYS, "CAN I STEAL YOU FOR A SECOND?"	A CHAMPAGNE GLASS APPEARS	THE BACHELOR GIVES SOMEONE HIS JACKET	SOMEONE SAYS THE WORD "PROCESS"
SOMEONE WEARS A GOLD DRESS	SOMEONE SAYS THE WORD "AMAZING"	SOMEONE SAYS THE WORD "IMPRESSION"	SOMEONE CRIES!	FIRST KISS OF THE SEASON

FUN FACT: Minnesota and Utah are the two states that have the greatest number of Google searches for "The Bachelor."

CUT ON DOTTED LINE TO USE THIS BINGO BOARD!

The
BACHELOR
Bingo

THIS BINGO CARD IS GOOD FOR THE PREMIER EPISODE OF "THE BACHELOR."

CUT ON DOTTED LINE TO USE THIS BINGO BOARD!

SOMEONE WEARS A YELLOW DRESS	THE BACHELOR PICKS UP THE FIRST IMPRESSION ROSE	SOMEONE LOOKS OVER THEIR SHOULDER	SOMEONE GETS INJURED	SOMEONE WEARS A BLINDFOLD
SOMEONE GETS OUT OF THE LIMO	SOMEONE TRIPS AS THEY WALK TO MEET THE BACHELOR	SOMEONE IS UNDER A BLANKET OUTSIDE	SOMEONE SAYS THEY "LOOK FORWARD" TO TALKING	SOMEONE SAYS THEY HAVE A CHILD
SOMEONE MENTIONS WANTING MARRIAGE	SOMEONE SAYS THE BACHELOR IS "HOT"	This free space isn't here to make friends.	SOMEONE TALKS ABOUT THEIR JOB BACK HOME	SOMEONE MENTIONS AN EX
SOMEONE SAYS, "CAN I STEAL YOU FOR A SECOND?"	SOMEONE SAYS THE WORD "AMAZING"	SOMEONE SAYS, "I'LL SEE YOU INSIDE"	HOST: "THIS IS THE FINAL ROSE TONIGHT"	TWO WOMEN GOSSIP ABOUT ANOTHER
A WOMAN CALLS ANOTHER WOMAN "BEAUTIFUL"	SOMEONE DABS THEIR EYES WITH A TISSUE	SOMEONE TALKS ABOUT CHARITY WORK	SOMEONE SAYS THE WORD "JOURNEY"	SOMEONE KISSES BACHELOR IN FRONT OF OTHERS

FUN FACT: Teachers and realtors are the most common professions among Bachelor contestants.

The
BACHELOR
Bingo

SOMEONE WEARS A PINK DRESS	SOMEONE SPIES ON THE BACHELOR THROUGH A WINDOW	HOST REMINDS BACHELOR THAT "HE'S IN CHARGE"	THE BACHELOR HOLDS HANDS WITH SOMEONE	SOMEONE JUMPS IN THE POOL
SOMEONE SAYS THE WORD "JOURNEY"	SOMEONE TRIPS WHILE WALKING	SOMEONE PLANS TO INTERRUPT THE BACHELOR	SOMEONE SAYS, "I'LL SEE YOU INSIDE"	SOMEONE TALKS ABOUT AN EX
THE BACHELOR CLINKS GLASSES WITH SOMEONE	SOMEONE SITS ON THE STAIRS	This free space isn't here to make friends.	EVERYONE RAISES THEIR GLASSES	YOU SEE A PALM TREE
SOMEONE WEARS A RED DRESS	SOMEONE ROLLS THEIR EYES	SOMEONE SAYS "RIGHT REASONS"	SOMEONE MENTIONS THEIR PARENTS' MARRIAGE	SOMEONE SAYS THEY WANT TO "FIND LOVE"
SOMEONE TALKS ABOUT WANTING CHILDREN	SOMEONE GETS INJURED	SOMEONE MENTIONS A 2-ON-1 DATE	SOMEONE TOUCHES THE BACHELOR'S LEG	SOMEONE APOLOGIZES FOR CRYING

QUOTABLE: "I'm, like, befumbled."
—*Hannah Brown, inventing her own vocabulary on Colton's season.*

CUT ON DOTTED LINE TO USE THIS BINGO BOARD!

The BACHELOR *Bingo*

THIS BINGO CARD IS GOOD FOR THE PREMIER EPISODE OF "THE BACHELOR."

SOMEONE TALKS ABOUT THEIR PET	SOMEONE INTERRUPTS A CONVERSATION	SOMEONE WEARS A RED DRESS	SOMEONE SAYS THE WORD "WEDDING"	SOMEONE MENTIONS AN EX
SOMEONE GIVES A HIGH FIVE	THE BACHELOR HOLDS HANDS WITH SOMEONE	SOMEONE TOUCHES THE BACHELOR'S LEG	THE BACHELOR STROLLS, LOOKING PENSIVE	SOMEONE CRIES
HOST: "THIS IS THE FINAL ROSE TONIGHT"	SOMEONE LOOKS OVER THEIR SHOULDER	This free space isn't here to make friends.	SOMEONE SAYS, "CAN I STEAL YOU FOR A SECOND?"	SOMEONE SAYS THE WORD "CONNECTION"
SOMEONE TRASH TALKS ANOTHER CONTESTANT	SOMEONE DECIDES TO LEAVE THE SHOW	EVERYONE SCREAMS WHEN THE BACHELOR SHOWS UP	SOMEONE SAYS, "I SAID I WOULDN'T CRY"	THE HOST FIRST APPEARS
SOMEONE SAYS "DRAMATIC"	SOMEONE TOUCHES THE BACHELOR'S ARM	SOMEONE ASKS TO TALK TO THE BACHELOR AT ROSE CEREMONY	SOMEONE PRIMPS IN THE MIRROR	SOMEONE SPIES THROUGH A WINDOW

FUN FACT: The roses for each rose ceremony are stored in a trash can on ice.

The BACHELOR Bingo

BACHELOR KISSES MORE THAN ONE PERSON ON NIGHT ONE	THE BACHELOR SAYS HIS "WIFE IS IN THIS ROOM"	SOMEONE HAS A SOUTHERN ACCENT	SOMEONE SAYS "MY PERSON"	SOMEONE WEARS A WHITE DRESS
A ROSE APPEARS ON SCREEN	SOMEONE SAYS THAT "FAMILY IS IMPORTANT"	BACHELOR GIVES FIRST IMPRESSION ROSE	SOMEONE KISSES BACHELOR ON CHEEK	BACHELOR SAYS SOMEONE ISN'T "READY" FOR MARRIAGE
SOMEONE SAYS THE WORD "CONNECTION"	YOU SEE A GLASS OF RED WINE	This free space isn't here to make friends.	SOMEONE FORGETS TO GIVE THEIR NAME	SOMEONE LOOKS OVER THEIR SHOULDER
SOMEONE PEERS OUT A LIMO WINDOW	SOMEONE TALKS ABOUT THEIR PARENTS' DIVORCE	SOMEONE WEARS A SILVER DRESS	SOMEONE SAYS THE BACHELOR IS "SEXY"	SOMEONE MAKES ROOM ON THE COUCH
SOMEONE GRABS THE BACHELOR'S HAND	SOMEONE TOUCHES THE BACHELOR'S LEG	SOMEONE TAKES A SIP OF THEIR DRINK	SOMEONE IS VISIBLY SWEATING	SOMEONE SAYS THE WORD " SPECIAL"

FUN FACT: You can stay at the Bachelor Mansion yourself by booking it on Airbnb.

CUT ON DOTTED LINE TO USE THIS BINGO BOARD!

The BACHELOR *Bingo*

THIS BINGO CARD IS GOOD FOR THE PREMIER EPISODE OF "THE BACHELOR."

CUT ON DOTTED LINE TO USE THIS BINGO BOARD!

SOMEONE FORGETS TO GIVE THEIR NAME	FIRST KISS OF THE SEASON	SOMEONE ROLLS THEIR EYES	SOMEONE PRIMPS IN THE MIRROR	SOMEONE TALKS ABOUT THEIR DOG
SOMEONE MENTIONS A BROTHER OR SISTER	SOMEONE TALKS ABOUT A BAD BREAK-UP	THE BACHELOR SAYS HIS "WIFE IS IN THIS ROOM"	SOMEONE MENTIONS A PREVIOUS SEASON	SOMEONE CLINKS/TAPS A GLASS TO GET ATTENTION
SOMEONE TALKS ABOUT A TRAGIC EVENT IN THEIR LIFE	A WOMAN TALKS TO CAMERA WHILE HOLDING ROSE	This free space isn't here to make friends.	SOMEONE SAYS THEY "CAN'T WAIT"	SOMEONE WEARS A BLACK DRESS
SOMEONE HAS A SOUTHERN ACCENT	TWO WOMEN HUG	TWO WOMEN TALK BEHIND ANOTHER'S BACK	SOMEONE TALKS ABOUT WHAT THEY GAVE UP TO BE HERE	SOMEONE MENTIONS THEIR CAREER
SOMEONE SAYS THEY WANT CHILDREN	A LIMO PULLS UP	SOMEONE SAYS "COMMITMENT"	SOMEONE SAYS THEY ARE "SCARED"	SOMEONE SAYS "MY PERSON"

FUN FACT: The production teams hoses down the driveway with water before filming to make it look shiny.

The BACHELOR *Bingo*

THIS BINGO CARD IS GOOD FOR THE PREMIER EPISODE OF "THE BACHELOR."

SOMEONE TALKS ABOUT A BAD BREAK-UP	SOMEONE SAYS THE BACHELOR WOULD BE A GREAT DAD	SOMEONE SAYS, "I'LL SEE YOU INSIDE"	THE HOST APPEARS	SOMEONE CLINKS/TAPS A GLASS TO GET ATTENTION
THE BACHELOR SAYS HE IS NERVOUS	SOMEONE MENTIONS A PREVIOUS SEASON	SOMEONE SAYS THE WORD "EXCITED"	SOMEONE ROLLS THEIR EYES	SOMEONE WEARS A STRAPLESS DRESS
SOMEONE TALKS ABOUT WHAT THEY GAVE UP TO BE HERE	SOMEONE FEEDS THE BACHELOR SOMETHING	This free space isn't here to make friends.	SPORTS ARE MENTIONED OR PLAYED	A WOMAN TALKS TO CAMERA WHILE HOLDING ROSE
SOMEONE COMPLAINS THEIR TIME WAS TOO SHORT	WOMAN SITS ON THE STAIRS	BACHELOR SITS ON A COUCH OUTSIDE	TWO WOMEN HUG	THE BACHELOR SAYS HIS "WIFE IS IN THIS ROOM"
TWO WOMEN TALK BEHIND ANOTHER'S BACK	SOMEONE SAYS "NOT HERE TO MAKE FRIENDS"	SOMEONE SAYS THE WORD "SURPRISED"	SOMEONE MENTIONS A BROTHER OR SISTER	SOMEONE MENTIONS THEIR CAREER

FUN FACT: Jesse Csincsak (Deanna) was the first to receive a first impression rose and eventually win.

CUT ON DOTTED LINE TO USE THIS BINGO BOARD!

The BACHELOR *Bingo*

THIS BINGO CARD IS GOOD FOR THE PREMIER EPISODE OF "THE BACHELOR."

CUT ON DOTTED LINE TO USE THIS BINGO BOARD!

SOMEONE SAYS "COMMITMENT"	SOMEONE TALKS ABOUT THEIR HOMETOWN	SOMEONE SAYS THE BACHELOR IS "CUTE"	THE HOST AND THE BACHELOR HAVE A SIT-DOWN	SOMEONE MENTIONS A BROTHER OR SISTER
THE BACHELOR SAYS HIS "WIFE IS IN THIS ROOM"	A LIMO ARRIVES	SOMEONE TALKS IN BABY VOICE	FIRST KISS OF THE SEASON	SOMEONE SAYS THEY ARE "SCARED"
SOMEONE WEARS A DRESS WITH SEQUINS	WOMAN IS ANNOYED SHE WAS INTERRUPTED	This free space isn't here to make friends.	SOMEONE SAYS THEY WANT CHILDREN	TWO WOMEN TALK BEHIND ANOTHER'S BACK
SOMEONE MENTIONS GETTING ENGAGED AT THE END	SOMEONE TRIPS	SOMEONE WEARS A SILLY COSTUME	SOMEONE MAKES THE BACHELOR LAUGH	SOMEONE TALKS ABOUT A TRAGIC EVENT IN THEIR LIFE
SOMEONE SAYS THE BACHELOR WOULD BE A GREAT DAD	SOMEONE MENTIONS THEIR CAREER	SOMEONE SAYS THE WORD "BUTTERFLIES"	SOMEONE SAYS THEY ARE "CONFIDENT"	SOMEONE IS SHOWN IN BATHROOM

FUN FACT: Limo arrival dresses must be approved by production.

The BACHELOR Bingo

SOMEONE SAYS THE WORD "JOURNEY"	SOMEONE SHARES A PERSONAL SOB STORY	SOMEONE KISSES THE BACHELOR IN FRONT OF OTHERS	SOMEONE JUMPS INTO THE BACHELOR'S ARMS	SOMEONE ACTUALLY TAKES A BITE OF FOOD
SOMEONE HAS TOO MUCH TO DRINK	THERE'S A POOL PARTY WITH THE BACHELOR	HOST: "THIS IS THE FINAL ROSE TONIGHT"	COMMERCIAL SHOWN FOR BACHELOR CASTING	THERE'S A 2-ON-1 DATE
YOU SEE A GLASS OF WHITE WINE	EVERYONE SCREAMS WHEN THE BACHELOR SHOWS UP	Will you accept this free space?	SOMEONE GETS JEWELRY ON A DATE	SOMEONE APPEARS IN A BIKINI
THE BACHELOR CANCELS COCKTAIL PARTY	SOMEONE SAYS, "CAN I STEAL YOU FOR A SECOND?"	RANDOM CELEBRITY APPEARANCE	FIREWORKS ARE ON A DATE	SOMEONE SAYS THE WORD "PROCESS"
SOMEONE WEARS A GOLD DRESS	SOMEONE SAYS THE WORD "AMAZING"	SOMEONE COMPLAINS ABOUT NOT GETTING A 1-ON-1	SOMEONE CRIES!	A DATE INVOLVES A HELICOPTER RIDE

FUN FACT: Rhonda from season 1 was the first person on the show to say, "I'm not here to make friends."

CUT ON DOTTED LINE TO USE THIS BINGO BOARD!

The BACHELOR *Bingo*

THIS BINGO CARD IS GOOD FOR ANY REGULAR SEASON EPISODE OF "THE BACHELOR."

CUT ON DOTTED LINE TO USE THIS BINGO BOARD!

SOMEONE WEARS A GOLD DRESS	BACHELOR SAYS "I DIDN'T EXPECT"	OTHER WOMEN SEE FIREWORKS FROM A DATE	SOMEONE GETS INJURED	THE BACHELOR CANCELS COCKTAIL PARTY
A GROUP DATE ROSE IS GIVEN	SOMEONE GETS A DRESS/OUTFIT ON A DATE	YOU SEE A GLASS OF WHITE WINE	SOMEONE COMPLAINS ABOUT NOT GETTING A 1-ON-1	A GROUP DATE INVOLVES PERFORMING ON STAGE
A HOT TUB APPEARS	RANDOM CELEBRITY APPEARANCE	Will you accept this free space?	SOMEONE TALKS ABOUT THEIR JOB BACK HOME	SOMEONE MENTIONS AN EX
SOMEONE SAYS, "CAN I STEAL YOU FOR A SECOND?"	SOMEONE SAYS THE WORD "AMAZING"	SOMEONE ACTUALLY TAKES A BITE OF FOOD	HOST: "THIS IS THE FINAL ROSE TONIGHT"	THERE'S A 2-ON-1 DATE
SOMEONE JUMPS INTO THE BACHELOR'S ARMS	SOMEONE DABS THEIR EYES WITH A TISSUE	SOMEONE TALKS ABOUT A NIECE OR NEPHEW	SOMEONE SAYS THE WORD "JOURNEY"	SOMEONE KISSES BACHELOR IN FRONT OF OTHERS

FUN FACT: Producers don't like contestants wearing patterned clothes on the show – they prefer solids.

The BACHELOR *Bingo*

THIS BINGO CARD IS GOOD FOR ANY REGULAR SEASON EPISODE OF "THE BACHELOR."

SOMEONE WEARS A PINK SHIRT	THERE'S A POOL PARTY WITH THE BACHELOR	HOST REMINDS BACHELOR THAT "HE'S IN CHARGE"	THE BACHELOR HOLDS HANDS WITH SOMEONE	THE BACHELOR CLIMBS IN THE HOT TUB
SOMEONE SAYS THE WORD "JOURNEY"	RANDOM CELEBRITY APPEARANCE	SOMEONE PLANS TO INTERRUPT THE BACHELOR	BACHELOR SAYS "I DIDN'T EXPECT"	SOMEONE TALKS ABOUT AN EX
THE BACHELOR CLINKS GLASSES WITH SOMEONE	FOOD IS SHOWN ON THE TABLE BUT NO ONE EATS	Will you accept this free space?	COCKTAIL PARTY BEGINS	YOU SEE A PALM TREE
SOMEONE WEARS A RED BATHING SUIT	COMMERCIAL SHOWN FOR BACHELOR CASTING	SOMEONE SAYS "RIGHT REASONS"	A GROUP DATE INVOLVES PERFORMING ON STAGE	SOMEONE SAYS THEY WANT TO "FIND LOVE"
SOMEONE TALKS ABOUT WANTING CHILDREN	SOMEONE GETS INJURED	SOMEONE MENTIONS A 2-ON-1 DATE	SOMEONE TALKS ABOUT THEIR PARENTS	SOMEONE APOLOGIZES FOR CRYING

FUN FACT: The mansion where the show is filmed is named Mansion Villa de la Vina.

CUT ON DOTTED LINE TO USE THIS BINGO BOARD!

The
BACHELOR
Bingo

SOMEONE TALKS ABOUT THEIR PET	THE BACHELOR DRIVES A CAR ON A DATE	SOMEONE WEARS A RED DRESS	SOMEONE SAYS THE WORD "WEDDING"	SOMEONE MENTIONS AN EX
SOMEONE GIVES A HIGH FIVE	THE BACHELOR HOLDS HANDS WITH SOMEONE	A DATE INVOLVES A HELICOPTER RIDE	THE BACHELOR STROLLS, LOOKING PENSIVE	SOMEONE CRIES AT A COCKTAIL PARTY
HOST: "THIS IS THE FINAL ROSE TONIGHT"	SOMEONE COMPLAINS ABOUT NOT GETTING A 1-ON-1	Will you accept this free space?	SOMEONE SAYS, "CAN I STEAL YOU FOR A SECOND?"	RANDOM CELEBRITY APPEARANCE
SOMEONE TRASH TALKS ANOTHER CONTESTANT	SOMEONE DECIDES TO LEAVE THE SHOW	EVERYONE SCREAMS WHEN THE BACHELOR SHOWS UP	SOMEONE SAYS, "I SAID I WOULDN'T CRY"	THE HOST FIRST APPEARS
SOMEONE SAYS "DRAMATIC"	SOMEONE TOUCHES THE BACHELOR'S ARM	SOMEONE ASKS TO TALK TO THE BACHELOR AT ROSE CEREMONY	SOMEONE PRIMPS IN THE MIRROR	A CELEBRITY GUEST APPEARS

FUN FACT: Jesse Palmer once hosted a baking competition
show on the Food Network.

The BACHELOR *Bingo*

THIS BINGO CARD IS GOOD FOR ANY REGULAR SEASON EPISODE OF "THE BACHELOR."

CUT ON DOTTED LINE TO USE THIS BINGO BOARD!

FIRST KISS OF THE EPISODE	THE BACHELOR SAYS HIS "WIFE IS IN THIS ROOM"	SOMEONE HAS A SOUTHERN ACCENT	SOMEONE SAYS "MY PERSON"	SOMEONE WEARS A WHITE DRESS
A ROSE APPEARS ON SCREEN	SOMEONE SAYS THAT "FAMILY IS IMPORTANT"	A DATE CARD ARRIVES	COMMERCIAL SHOWN FOR BACHELOR CASTING	BACHELOR SAYS SOMEONE ISN'T "READY" FOR MARRIAGE
SOMEONE SAYS THE WORD "CONNECTION"	YOU SEE A GLASS OF RED WINE	Will you accept this free space?	A GROUP DATE ROSE IS GIVEN	SOMEONE WEARS A TANK TOP
EVERYONE SCREAMS WHEN THE BACHELOR SHOWS UP	SOMEONE TALKS ABOUT THEIR PARENTS' DIVORCE	SOMEONE WEARS A SILVER DRESS	SOMEONE SAYS THE BACHELOR IS "SEXY"	THEY GO HORSE BACK RIDING ON A DATE
SOMEONE JUMPS INTO THE BACHELOR'S ARMS	THE BACHELOR ANNOUNCES A NEW CITY/ COUNTRY	SOMEONE TAKES A SIP OF THEIR DRINK	SOMEONE IS VISIBLY SWEATING	RANDOM MUSICAL ACT PERFORMS ON A DATE

FUN FACT: In 2010, Neil Lane partnered with Kay Jewelers to create a bridal collection.

The BACHELOR *Bingo*

THIS BINGO CARD IS GOOD FOR ANY REGULAR SEASON EPISODE OF "THE BACHELOR."

CUT ON DOTTED LINE TO USE THIS BINGO BOARD!

SOMEONE KISSES BACHELOR IN FRONT OF OTHERS	FIRST KISS OF THE EPISODE	A DATE CARD ARRIVES	SOMEONE PRIMPS IN THE MIRROR	SOMEONE TALKS ABOUT THEIR DOG
SOMEONE MENTIONS A BROTHER OR SISTER	SOMEONE TALKS ABOUT A BAD BREAK-UP	THE BACHELOR SAYS HIS "WIFE IS IN THIS ROOM"	SOMEONE MENTIONS A PREVIOUS SEASON	SOMEONE CLINKS/TAPS A GLASS TO GET ATTENTION
SOMEONE TALKS ABOUT A TRAGIC EVENT IN THEIR LIFE	A WOMAN TALKS TO CAMERA WHILE HOLDING ROSE	Will you accept this free space?	SOMEONE SAYS THEY "CAN'T WAIT"	SOMEONE WEARS A BLACK DRESS
RANDOM MUSICAL ACT PERFORMS ON A DATE	TWO WOMEN HUG	TWO WOMEN TALK BEHIND ANOTHER'S BACK	SOMEONE TALKS ABOUT WHAT THEY GAVE UP TO BE HERE	SOMEONE MENTIONS THEIR CAREER
SOMEONE SAYS THEY WANT CHILDREN	SOMEONE MENTIONS BEING MARRIED BEFORE	SOMEONE SAYS "COMMITMENT"	SOMEONE SAYS THEY ARE "SCARED"	SOMEONE SAYS "MY PERSON"

FUN FACT: In season one of "The Bachelorette," a candle floating in a pool lit a plant on fire during Trista Rehn and Ryan Sutter's proposal.

The BACHELOR *Bingo*

THIS BINGO CARD IS GOOD FOR ANY REGULAR SEASON EPISODE OF "THE BACHELOR."

SOMEONE TALKS ABOUT A BAD BREAK-UP	SOMEONE SAYS THE BACHELOR WOULD BE A GREAT DAD	SOMEONE TALKS ABOUT A TRAGIC EVENT IN THEIR LIFE	COMMERCIAL SHOWN FOR BACHELOR CASTING	SOMEONE CLINKS/TAPS A GLASS TO GET ATTENTION
THE BACHELOR SAYS HE IS NERVOUS	SOMEONE MENTIONS A PREVIOUS SEASON	SOMEONE SAYS THE WORD "EXCITED"	SOMEONE RIDES ON A TRAIN OR TROLLEY	SOMEONE WEARS A STRAPLESS DRESS
SOMEONE TALKS ABOUT WHAT THEY GAVE UP TO BE HERE	THEY FEED EACH OTHER ON A DATE	*Will you accept this free space?*	SOMEONE MENTIONS BEING MARRIED BEFORE	A WOMAN TALKS TO CAMERA WHILE HOLDING ROSE
THE WOMEN GRILL THE PERSON WHO RETURNED FROM A DATE	WOMAN DOESN'T WANT TO DISCUSS DATE	WOMAN SHOWN PACKING	TWO WOMEN HUG	THE BACHELOR SAYS HIS "WIFE IS IN THIS ROOM"
TWO WOMEN TALK BEHIND ANOTHER'S BACK	SOMEONE WEARS A TANK TOP	SUITCASE IS REMOVED BY PRODUCTION	RANDOM MUSICAL ACT PERFORMS ON A DATE	SOMEONE MENTIONS THEIR CAREER

FUN FACT: Contestants are not allowed to run for public office for one year after appearing on the show.

CUT ON DOTTED LINE TO USE THIS BINGO BOARD!

The
BACHELOR
Bingo

RANDOM MUSICAL ACT PERFORMS ON A DATE	SOMEONE TALKS ABOUT CHARITY WORK	SOMEONE SAYS THE BACHELOR IS "CUTE"	THE HOST AND THE BACHELOR HAVE A SIT-DOWN	SOMEONE MENTIONS A BROTHER OR SISTER
THE BACHELOR SAYS HIS "WIFE IS IN THIS ROOM"	A DATE CARD ARRIVES	SOMEONE TALKS IN BABY VOICE	FIRST KISS OF THE EPISODE	SOMEONE SAYS THEY ARE "SCARED"
SOMEONE WEARS A DRESS WITH SEQUINS	WOMAN DOESN'T WANT TO DISCUSS DATE	*Will you accept this free space?*	SOMEONE SAYS THEY WANT CHILDREN	TWO WOMEN TALK BEHIND ANOTHER'S BACK
WOMAN SHOWN PACKING	SOMEONE WEARS SNEAKERS	A MICROPHONE IS SHOWN	SOMEONE SAYS THE BACHELOR IS FUNNY	SOMEONE TALKS ABOUT A TRAGIC EVENT IN THEIR LIFE
SOMEONE SAYS THE BACHELOR WOULD BE A GREAT DAD	SOMEONE MENTIONS THEIR CAREER	SOMEONE SAYS THE WORD "BUTTERFLIES"	SUITCASE IS REMOVED BY PRODUCTION	THE WOMEN GRILL THE PERSON WHO RETURNED FROM A DATE

QUOTABLE: "Michael Jordan took naps. Abe Lincoln took naps. Why am I getting in trouble for napping?" –*Corinne Olympios after taking a nap at a rose ceremony.*

CUT ON DOTTED LINE TO USE THIS BINGO BOARD!

The BACHELOR *Bingo*

THIS BINGO CARD IS GOOD FOR THE HOMETOWN DATES EPISODE.

SOMEONE SAYS THE WORD "JOURNEY"	THE BACHELOR MEETS SOMEONE'S DOG	THE BACHELOR ARRIVES IN THE FIRST HOMETOWN	SOMEONE JUMPS INTO THE BACHELOR'S ARMS	A WOMAN LISTS WHO THE BACHELOR WILL BE MEETING
SOMEONE'S PARENTS ARE SITTING ON A COUCH	SOMEONE SAYS "I'LL MISS YOU"	HOST: "THIS IS THE FINAL ROSE TONIGHT"	THE HOST FIRST APPEARS	THE BACHELOR MEETS A BROTHER OR SISTER
A FAMILY SITS DOWN TO DINNER	THEY VISIT A LOCAL RESTAURANT IN A HOMETOWN	Most Dramatic. Free Space. Ever.	SOMEONE SAYS: "ARE YOU READY TO BE ENGAGED?"	A FAMILY IS CONCERNED ABOUT THE OTHER WOMEN
A PARENT IS SKEPTICAL ABOUT THE SHOW	BACHELOR SAYS HE'S "FALLING IN LOVE"	THE BACHELOR MEETS SOMEONE'S FRIENDS	BACHELOR SAYS IT'S THE "HARDEST DECISION YET"	SOMEONE SAYS THE WORD "PROCESS"
SOMEONE SAYS THEY CAN SEE THE BACHELOR "IN THE FAMILY"	SOMEONE SAYS THE WORD "AMAZING"	SOMEONE SAYS THE WORD "IMPRESSION"	SOMEONE CRIES!	BACHELOR DESCRIBES WHAT HE LIKES ABOUT ONE OF THE WOMEN

FUN FACT: A family actually owns the Bachelor mansion – they vacate for filming.

The BACHELOR Bingo

THIS BINGO CARD IS GOOD FOR THE HOMETOWN DATES EPISODE.

SOMEONE SHOWS THEIR CHILDHOOD BEDROOM	THE CAR DOOR SHUTS AFTER SOMEONE SAYS GOODBYE	A WOMAN LISTS WHO THE BACHELOR WILL BE MEETING	A PARENT DISAPPROVES OF THE RELATIONSHIP	SOMEONE SAYS THEY'RE ALMOST AT "THE END"
SOMEONE GIVES FLOWERS	SOMEONE SAYS "I'LL MISS YOU"	BACHELOR SAYS HE'S "FALLING IN LOVE"	A FAMILY IS CONCERNED ABOUT THE OTHER WOMEN	SOMEONE SAYS THE CITY THEY'RE IN IS "BEAUTIFUL"
SOMEONE MENTIONS WANTING MARRIAGE	SOMEONE SAYS THE BACHELOR IS "HOT"	Most Dramatic. Free Space. Ever.	SOMEONE TALKS ABOUT THEIR JOB BACK HOME	SOMEONE MENTIONS AN EX
A PET OTHER THAN A CAT OR DOG IS SHOWN	SOMEONE SAYS THE WORD "AMAZING"	SOMEONE DOESN'T THINK YOU COULD FALL IN LOVE SO FAST	HOST: "THIS IS THE FINAL ROSE TONIGHT"	THEY VISIT A LOCAL RESTAURANT IN A HOMETOWN
SOMEONE SAYS THEY CAN SEE THE BACHELOR "IN THE FAMILY"	THE BACHELOR ASKS A WOMAN IF SHE HAS ANY "QUESTIONS"	THE BACHELOR ARRIVES IN THE FIRST HOMETOWN	SOMEONE SAYS THE WORD "JOURNEY"	SOMEONE KISSES BACHELOR IN FRONT OF OTHERS

FUN FACT: As Bachelor, Jesse Palmer gave a woman a rose by accident after mixing up names.

The BACHELOR *Bingo*

THE BACHELOR HOLDS THE DOOR OPEN FOR SOMEONE	A FAMILY SITS DOWN TO DINNER	THE FIRST WOMAN ARRIVES AT THE ROSE CEREMONY	THE BACHELOR HOLDS HANDS WITH SOMEONE	SOMEONE GIVES FLOWERS
SOMEONE SAYS THE WORD "JOURNEY"	THE BACHELOR ASKS A WOMAN IF SHE HAS ANY "QUESTIONS"	THE CAR DOOR SHUTS AFTER SOMEONE SAYS GOODBYE	SOMEONE SAYS THEY CAN SEE THE BACHELOR "IN THE FAMILY"	THE BACHELOR COMPLIMENTS THE MOTHER
THE BACHELOR CLINKS GLASSES WITH SOMEONE	SOMEONE SAYS: "ARE YOU READY TO BE ENGAGED?"	Most Dramatic. Free Space. Ever.	A TOAST HAPPENS AT DINNER	THE BACHELOR MEETS SOMEONE'S DOG
SOMEONE RUNS TO GREET THE BACHELOR	THE BACHELOR MEETS SOMEONE'S FRIENDS	SOMEONE SAYS "RIGHT REASONS"	SOMEONE MENTIONS THEIR PARENTS' MARRIAGE	SOMEONE SAYS THEY WANT TO "FIND LOVE"
SOMEONE TALKS ABOUT WANTING CHILDREN	THE BACHELOR TALKS TO THE FATHER ONE-ON-ONE	SOMEONE'S PARENTS ARE SITTING ON A COUCH	SOMEONE TOUCHES THE BACHELOR'S LEG	SOMEONE APOLOGIZES FOR CRYING

FUN FACT: Ben Higgins and Lauren Bushnell got engaged on "The Bachelor" and later starred in their own reality show, "Ben & Lauren: Happily Ever After?"

CUT ON DOTTED LINE TO USE THIS BINGO BOARD!

The BACHELOR Bingo

THIS BINGO CARD IS GOOD FOR THE HOMETOWN DATES EPISODE.

CUT ON DOTTED LINE TO USE THIS BINGO BOARD!

SOMEONE PLAYS WITH THEIR PET	SOMEONE SAYS THEY CAN SEE THE BACHELOR "IN THE FAMILY"	BACHELOR DESCRIBES WHAT HE LIKES ABOUT ONE OF THE WOMEN	THE FIRST WOMAN ARRIVES AT THE ROSE CEREMONY	SOMEONE MENTIONS AN EX
SOMEONE SAYS THEY'RE ALMOST AT "THE END"	THE BACHELOR HOLDS HANDS WITH SOMEONE	SOMEONE TOUCHES THE BACHELOR'S LEG	THE BACHELOR STROLLS, LOOKING PENSIVE	SOMEONE SHOWS THEIR CHILDHOOD BEDROOM
HOST: "THIS IS THE FINAL ROSE TONIGHT"	A FAMILY IS CONCERNED ABOUT THE OTHER WOMEN	Most Dramatic. Free Space. Ever.	BACHELOR SAYS IT'S THE "HARDEST DECISION YET"	SOMEONE SAYS THE WORD "CONNECTION"
A PARENT DISAPPROVES OF THE RELATIONSHIP	THE BACHELOR MEETS A BROTHER OR SISTER	SOMEONE SAYS "I'LL MISS YOU"	SOMEONE SAYS, "I SAID I WOULDN'T CRY"	THE BACHELOR TALKS TO THE FATHER ONE-ON-ONE
SOMEONE SAYS "DRAMATIC"	SOMEONE TOUCHES THE BACHELOR'S ARM	SOMEONE ASKS TO TALK TO THE BACHELOR AT ROSE CEREMONY	SOMEONE DOESN'T THINK YOU COULD FALL IN LOVE SO FAST	SOMEONE SAYS: "ARE YOU READY TO BE ENGAGED?"

QUOTABLE: "I'm so disgusted with you. You sold me out ...
and then flirted with me all weekend. We'll get to your lying issues in a minute."
– *Jake Pavelka to Vienna Girardi on their own awkward break-up special*

The BACHELOR *Bingo*

THIS BINGO CARD IS GOOD FOR THE HOMETOWN DATES EPISODE.

CUT ON DOTTED LINE TO USE THIS BINGO BOARD!

SOMEONE SAYS THE CITY THEY'RE IN IS "BEAUTIFUL"	A PARENT DISAPPROVES OF THE RELATIONSHIP	THE CAR DOOR SHUTS AFTER SOMEONE SAYS GOODBYE	SOMEONE SAYS "MY PERSON"	THE BACHELOR TALKS TO THE MOTHER ONE-ON-ONE
SOMEONE GIVES FLOWERS	SOMEONE SAYS THAT "FAMILY IS IMPORTANT"	THE FATHER GIVES HER BLESSING	THE BACHELOR PUTS HIS HAND ON SOMEONE'S KNEE	BACHELOR SAYS SOMEONE ISN'T "READY" FOR MARRIAGE
SOMEONE SAYS THE WORD "CONNECTION"	A SIBLING LOOKS ALMOST IDENTICAL TO ONE OF THE FINAL FOUR	Most Dramatic. Free Space. Ever.	A FAMILY SITS DOWN TO DINNER	THE BACHELOR ASKS A WOMAN IF SHE HAS ANY "QUESTIONS"
THE BACHELOR MEETS SOMEONE'S DOG	SOMEONE TALKS ABOUT THEIR PARENTS' DIVORCE	SOMEONE'S PARENTS ARE SITTING ON A COUCH	SOMEONE SAYS THE BACHELOR IS "PERFECT"	THEY VISIT A LOCAL RESTAURANT IN A HOMETOWN
SOMEONE GRABS THE BACHELOR'S HAND	SOMEONE TOUCHES THE BACHELOR'S LEG	SOMEONE TAKES A SIP OF THEIR DRINK	SOMEONE IS VISIBLY SWEATING	SOMEONE SAYS THE WORD "SPECIAL"

FUN FACT: Bachelor Ben Flajnik later dated Jennifer Love Hewitt.

The
BACHELOR
Bingo

SOMEONE FORGETS TO GIVE THEIR NAME	SOMEONE SAYS THEY'RE ALMOST AT "THE END"	SOMEONE ROLLS THEIR EYES	BACHELOR SAYS HE'S "FALLING IN LOVE"	SOMEONE PLAYS WITH THEIR DOG
THE BACHELOR MEETS A BROTHER OR SISTER	SOMEONE TALKS ABOUT A BAD BREAK-UP	THE BACHELOR TALKS TO THE MOTHER ONE-ON-ONE	SOMEONE MENTIONS A PREVIOUS SEASON	BACHELOR DESCRIBES WHAT HE LIKES ABOUT ONE OF THE WOMEN
SOMEONE TALKS ABOUT A TRAGIC EVENT IN THEIR LIFE	SOMEONE DOESN'T THINK YOU COULD FALL IN LOVE SO FAST	Most Dramatic. Free Space. Ever.	SOMEONE SAYS THEY "CAN'T WAIT"	A FAMILY IS CONCERNED ABOUT THE OTHER WOMEN
THEY VISIT A LOCAL RESTAURANT IN A HOMETOWN	THE BACHELOR MEETS SOMEONE'S FRIENDS	THE BACHELOR ARRIVES IN THE FIRST HOMETOWN	SOMEONE TALKS ABOUT WHAT THEY GAVE UP TO BE HERE	THE BACHELOR ASKS A WOMAN IF SHE HAS ANY "QUESTIONS"
SOMEONE SAYS THEY WANT CHILDREN	SOMEONE SAYS: "ARE YOU READY TO BE ENGAGED?"	SOMEONE SAYS "COMMITMENT"	SOMEONE SAYS THEY ARE "SCARED"	SOMEONE SAYS "MY PERSON"

FUN FACT: The Bachelor mansion almost burned down during wildfires in 2018.

CUT ON DOTTED LINE TO USE THIS BINGO BOARD!

The BACHELOR *Bingo*

SOMEONE TALKS ABOUT A BAD BREAK-UP	SOMEONE SAYS THE BACHELOR WOULD BE A GREAT DAD	SOMEONE TALKS ABOUT A TRAGIC EVENT IN THEIR LIFE	THE HOST APPEARS	BACHELOR SAYS HE'S "FALLING IN LOVE"
THE BACHELOR SAYS HE IS NERVOUS	SOMEONE MENTIONS A PREVIOUS SEASON	SOMEONE SAYS THE WORD "EXCITED"	THE BACHELOR PUTS HIS HAND ON SOMEONE'S KNEE	THE CAR DOOR SHUTS AFTER SOMEONE SAYS GOODBYE
SOMEONE TALKS ABOUT WHAT THEY GAVE UP TO BE HERE	A FAMILY SITS DOWN TO DINNER	Most Dramatic. Free Space. Ever.	BACHELOR SAYS IT'S THE "HARDEST DECISION YET"	THE BACHELOR COMPLIMENTS A MOTHER
THE FIRST WOMAN ARRIVES AT THE ROSE CEREMONY	SOMEONE DOESN'T THINK YOU COULD FALL IN LOVE SO FAST	SOMEONE SAYS: "ARE YOU READY TO BE ENGAGED?"	THE BACHELOR MEETS SOMEONE'S DOG	THE BACHELOR DESCRIBES WHAT HE LIKES ABOUT A WOMAN
SOMEONE'S PARENTS ARE SITTING ON A COUCH	SOMEONE SAYS "I'LL MISS YOU"	SOMEONE SAYS THE WORD "SURPRISED"	THE BACHELOR MEETS A BROTHER OR SISTER	SOMEONE TALKS ABOUT POSSIBLY MOVING

FUN FACT: Nick Viall is the only person to become a runner-up twice on the show.

The BACHELOR Bingo

THIS BINGO CARD IS GOOD FOR THE HOMETOWN DATES EPISODE.

SOMEONE SAYS "COMMITMENT"	THE BACHELOR ASKS A WOMAN IF SHE HAS ANY "QUESTIONS"	SOMEONE TALKS ABOUT POSSIBLY MOVING	THE HOST AND THE BACHELOR HAVE A SIT-DOWN	SOMEONE MENTIONS A BROTHER OR SISTER
THE BACHELOR SAYS HIS "WIFE IS IN THIS ROOM"	SOMEONE SAYS THEY'RE ALMOST AT "THE END"	SOMEONE TALKS IN BABY VOICE	SOMEONE SHOWS THEIR CHILDHOOD BEDROOM	SOMEONE SAYS THEY ARE "SCARED"
A PARENT SAYS, "I DON'T WANT TO SEE YOU GET HURT"	BACHELOR DESCRIBES WHAT HE LIKES ABOUT ONE OF THE WOMEN	Most Dramatic. Free Space. Ever.	SOMEONE SAYS THEY WANT CHILDREN	THE BACHELOR HAS A ONE-ON-ONE WITH A FATHER
SOMEONE MENTIONS GETTING ENGAGED AT THE END	THE BACHELOR MEETS A BROTHER OR SISTER	A FAMILY IS CONCERNED ABOUT THE OTHER WOMEN	SOMEONE MAKES THE BACHELOR LAUGH	SOMEONE TALKS ABOUT A TRAGIC EVENT IN THEIR LIFE
SOMEONE SAYS THE BACHELOR WOULD BE A GREAT DAD	SOMEONE SAYS THE CITY THEY'RE IN IS "BEAUTIFUL"	SOMEONE SAYS THE WORD "BUTTERFLIES"	SOMEONE SAYS THEY ARE "CONFIDENT"	THE BACHELOR MEETS SOMEONE'S FRIENDS

FUN FACT: Bachelorette Deanna Pappas later married the twin brother of a contestant from a different season.

CUT ON DOTTED LINE TO USE THIS BINGO BOARD!

The BACHELOR *Bingo*

THIS BINGO CARD IS GOOD FOR THE FANTASY SUITES EPISODE.

SOMEONE SAYS THE WORD "JOURNEY"	THE FANTASY SUITE CARD APPEARS	SOMEONE SAYS THEY FEEL "LUCKY"	SOMEONE JUMPS INTO THE BACHELOR'S ARMS	THERE ARE ROSE PETALS SCATTERED ABOUT
SOMEONE IS SHOWN WEARING A ROBE	THE COUPLE IS IN A HOT TUB	HOST: "THIS IS THE FINAL ROSE TONIGHT"	THE HOST FIRST APPEARS	SOMEONE SAYS THEY WOULD CONSIDER MOVING
HOST SAYS "OVERNIGHT DATES"	THE BACHELOR ENTERS THE ROOM	This free space is here for the right reasons.	THE COUPLE EXPLORES A STREET MARKET	SOMEONE SAYS GOODBYE FROM A HOTEL BALCONY
SOMEONE GIVES THE BACHELOR A GIFT	THE BACHELOR SAYS, "CAN I WALK YOU OUT?"	SOMEONE SAYS "OTHER GIRLS"	SOMEONE SAYS "MY BIGGEST FEAR"	SOMEONE SAYS THE WORD "PROCESS"
A WATERFALL IS SHOWN	SOMEONE SAYS THE WORD "AMAZING"	CLOTHES OR SHOES SHOWN ON HOTEL ROOM FLOOR	DO NOT DISTURB SIGN SHOWN ON DOOR	THE BACHELOR SAYS, "WHEN I WOKE UP THIS MORNING"

QUOTABLE: "I like the words you use. Words in general. Words that you use, how you speak. So proper."
—Bachelor Juan Pablo Galavis

CUT ON DOTTED LINE TO USE THIS BINGO BOARD!

The BACHELOR Bingo

THIS BINGO CARD IS GOOD FOR THE FANTASY SUITES EPISODE.

SOMEONE SAYS GOODBYE FROM A HOTEL BALCONY	SOMEONE SAYS THEY'RE "IN LOVE"	THE BACHELOR SAYS, "CAN I WALK YOU OUT?"	SOMEONE WEARS A BIKINI	THE COUPLE EXPLORES A STREET MARKET
THERE ARE ROSE PETALS SCATTERED ABOUT	SOMEONE SAYS THEY CAN'T MOVE TO ANOTHER CITY	CLOTHES OR SHOES SHOWN ON HOTEL ROOM FLOOR	THE COUPLE IS IN A HOT TUB	HOST SAYS "OVERNIGHT DATES"
SOMEONE MENTIONS WANTING AN ENGAGEMENT AT THE END	SOMEONE SAYS THE BACHELOR IS "HOT"	This free space is here for the right reasons.	SOMEONE TALKS ABOUT THEIR JOB BACK HOME	SOMEONE MENTIONS AN EX
SOMEONE SAYS THEY FEEL "LUCKY"	SOMEONE SAYS THE WORD "AMAZING"	SOMEONE ACTUALLY TAKES A BITE OF FOOD	HOST: "THIS IS THE FINAL ROSE TONIGHT"	THE BACHELOR ENTERS A HOTEL ROOM WITH SOMEONE
SOMEONE SAYS "OTHER GIRLS"	A WATERFALL IS SHOWN	THE BACHELOR SAYS, "WHEN I WOKE UP THIS MORNING"	SOMEONE SAYS THE WORD "JOURNEY"	SOMEONE KISSES BACHELOR IN FRONT OF OTHERS

FUN FACT: Carly Waddell was a bridesmaid in Jade Roper and Tanner Tolbert's wedding.

CUT ON DOTTED LINE TO USE THIS BINGO BOARD!

The
BACHELOR
Bingo

THE BACHELOR ENTERS A HOTEL ROOM WITH SOMEONE	THE BACHELOR SAYS, "CAN I WALK YOU OUT?"	HOST SAYS "OVERNIGHT DATES"	THE BACHELOR HOLDS HANDS WITH SOMEONE	THE FANTASY SUITE CARD APPEARS
SOMEONE SAYS THE WORD "JOURNEY"	SOMEONE WEARS A BIKINI	THERE ARE ROSE PETALS SCATTERED ABOUT	THE COUPLE EXPLORES A STREET MARKET	SOMEONE TALKS ABOUT AN EX
THE BACHELOR CLINKS GLASSES WITH SOMEONE	SOMEONE SAYS THEY'RE "IN LOVE"	This free space is here for the right reasons.	SOMEONE MENTIONS WANTING AN ENGAGEMENT AT THE END	SOMEONE IS SHOWN WEARING A ROBE
SOMEONE SAYS "MY BIGGEST FEAR"	CLOTHES OR SHOES SHOWN ON HOTEL ROOM FLOOR	SOMEONE SAYS "RIGHT REASONS"	SOMEONE MENTIONS THEIR PARENTS' MARRIAGE	SOMEONE SAYS THEY WANT TO "FIND LOVE"
SOMEONE TALKS ABOUT WANTING CHILDREN	THE BACHELOR SAYS, "WHEN I WOKE UP THIS MORNING"	SOMEONE SAYS THEY DON'T MIND MOVING	SOMEONE TOUCHES THE BACHELOR'S LEG	SOMEONE APOLOGIZES FOR CRYING

FUN FACT: Jillian Harris was the first woman from Canada to star as the Bachelorette in the United States.

CUT ON DOTTED LINE TO USE THIS BINGO BOARD!

The BACHELOR *Bingo*

THIS BINGO CARD IS GOOD FOR THE FANTASY SUITES EPISODE.

SOMEONE SAYS "MY BIGGEST FEAR"	THE BACHELOR ENTERS A HOTEL ROOM WITH SOMEONE	SOMEONE SAYS THEY CAN'T MOVE TO ANOTHER CITY	SOMEONE SAYS THE WORD "WEDDING"	THE COUPLE DOES AN ACTIVITY REQUIRING A HELMET
THE COUPLE IS IN A HOT TUB	THE COUPLE EATS BREAKFAST IN BED	SOMEONE TOUCHES THE BACHELOR'S LEG	THE BACHELOR STROLLS, LOOKING PENSIVE	THE BACHELOR SAYS SOMEONE WOULD BE A "GREAT WIFE"
HOST: "THIS IS THE FINAL ROSE TONIGHT"	SOMEONE MENTIONS WANTING AN ENGAGEMENT AT THE END	This free space is here for the right reasons.	SOMEONE SAYS THEY FEEL "LUCKY"	SOMEONE SAYS THE WORD "CONNECTION"
SOMEONE SAYS GOODBYE FROM A HOTEL BALCONY	SOMEONE DECIDES TO LEAVE THE SHOW	THERE ARE ROSE PETALS SCATTERED ABOUT	SOMEONE SAYS THEY'RE "IN LOVE"	THE HOST FIRST APPEARS
SOMEONE SAYS "DRAMATIC"	SOMEONE TOUCHES THE BACHELOR'S ARM	SOMEONE ASKS TO TALK TO THE BACHELOR AT ROSE CEREMONY	SOMEONE PRIMPS IN THE MIRROR	THE BEACH IS SHOWN

CUT ON DOTTED LINE TO USE THIS BINGO BOARD!

FUN FACT: Producers ask contestants to use the word "Journey" — that's why it's heard so often.

The BACHELOR *Bingo*

THIS BINGO CARD IS GOOD FOR THE FANTASY SUITES EPISODE.

CUT ON DOTTED LINE TO USE THIS BINGO BOARD!

CLOTHES OR SHOES SHOWN ON HOTEL ROOM FLOOR	THE BACHELOR SAYS HIS "WIFE IS IN THIS ROOM"	THERE IS A FIRE BURNING IN A FIREPLACE	SOMEONE SAYS "MY PERSON"	THE COUPLE DOES AN ACTIVITY REQUIRING A HELMET
DO NOT DISTURB SIGN SHOWN ON DOOR	SOMEONE SAYS THAT "FAMILY IS IMPORTANT"	THE BACHELOR SAYS SOMEONE WOULD BE A "GREAT WIFE"	SOMEONE SAYS GOODBYE FROM A HOTEL BALCONY	BACHELOR SAYS SOMEONE ISN'T "READY" FOR MARRIAGE
SOMEONE SAYS THE WORD "CONNECTION"	THE FANTASY SUITE CARD APPEARS	This free space is here for the right reasons.	SOMEONE IS SHOWN WEARING A ROBE	SOMEONE SAYS THEY CAN'T MOVE TO ANOTHER CITY
THERE ARE ROSE PETALS SCATTERED ABOUT	A WOMAN SPECULATES ABOUT THE BACHELOR'S OTHER DATES	SOMEONE SAYS THEY'RE "IN LOVE"	SOMEONE SAYS "OTHER GIRLS"	SOMEONE MENTIONS WANTING AN ENGAGEMENT AT THE END
THE BACHELOR SAYS, "CAN I WALK YOU OUT?"	SOMEONE TOUCHES THE BACHELOR'S LEG	SOMEONE TAKES A SIP OF THEIR DRINK	SOMEONE IS VISIBLY SWEATING	SOMEONE SAYS THE WORD "SPECIAL"

QUOTABLE: "Like, I'm done. Done. That was glitter. Glitter."
–Krystal Nielsen after getting eliminated

The BACHELOR *Bingo*

THIS BINGO CARD IS GOOD FOR THE FANTASY SUITES EPISODE.

THE BACHELOR ENTERS A HOTEL ROOM WITH SOMEONE	THERE IS A FIRE BURNING IN A FIREPLACE	SOMEONE SAYS THE WORD "TRUST"	SOMEONE PRIMPS IN THE MIRROR	THE FANTASY SUITE CARD APPEARS
THE COUPLE EATS BREAKFAST IN BED	SOMEONE TALKS ABOUT A BAD BREAK-UP	THE BACHELOR SAYS HIS "WIFE IS IN THIS ROOM"	SOMEONE SAYS "MY BIGGEST FEAR"	CLOTHES OR SHOES SHOWN ON HOTEL ROOM FLOOR
SOMEONE SAYS "OTHER GIRLS"	THE COUPLE IS IN A HOT TUB	This free space is here for the right reasons.	SOMEONE SAYS THEY "CAN'T WAIT"	A WOMAN SPECULATES ABOUT THE BACHELOR'S OTHER DATES
SOMEONE SAYS THEY CAN DO THEIR JOB "ANYWHERE"	SOMEONE SAYS THEY FEEL "LUCKY"	THE COUPLE DOES AN ACTIVITY REQUIRING A HELMET	THE BACHELOR SAYS SOMEONE WOULD BE A "GREAT WIFE"	SOMEONE MENTIONS THEIR CAREER
SOMEONE SAYS THEY WANT CHILDREN	SOMEONE IS SHOWN WEARING A ROBE	SOMEONE SAYS "COMMITMENT"	SOMEONE SAYS THEY ARE "SCARED"	SOMEONE SAYS "MY PERSON"

FUN FACT: After starring as Bachelorette, Trista Rehn appeared in a Brad Paisley music video.

The BACHELOR *Bingo*

THIS BINGO CARD IS GOOD FOR THE FANTASY SUITES EPISODE.

SOMEONE TALKS ABOUT A BAD BREAK-UP	SOMEONE SAYS THE BACHELOR WOULD BE A GREAT DAD	THE COUPLE DOES AN ACTIVITY REQUIRING A HELMET	THE HOST APPEARS	DO NOT DISTURB SIGN SHOWN ON DOOR
THE BACHELOR SAYS HE IS NERVOUS	THE BACHELOR CLOSES HOTEL ROOM DOOR TO BLOCK CAMERA	SOMEONE SAYS THE WORD "EXCITED"	SOMEONE SAYS THEY'RE "IN LOVE"	SOMEONE SAYS THEY CAN DO THEIR JOB "ANYWHERE"
SOMEONE TALKS ABOUT WANTING TO "BUILD A LIFE"	SOMEONE SAYS GOODBYE FROM A HOTEL BALCONY	This free space is here for the right reasons.	THERE IS A FIRE BURNING IN A FIREPLACE	THE BACHELOR SAYS SOMEONE WOULD BE A "GREAT WIFE"
CLOTHES OR SHOES SHOWN ON HOTEL ROOM FLOOR	THE FANTASY SUITE CARD APPEARS	A WOMAN SPECULATES ABOUT THE BACHELOR'S OTHER DATES	THE COUPLE EATS BREAKFAST IN BED	SOMEONE SAYS THEY FEEL "LUCKY"
SOMEONE MENTIONS WANTING AN ENGAGEMENT AT THE END	SOMEONE SAYS "OTHER GIRLS"	SOMEONE SAYS THE WORD "SURPRISED"	SOMEONE MENTIONS A BROTHER OR SISTER	THE FIRST WOMAN APPEARS AT THE ROSE CEREMONY

QUOTABLE: "Life ain't all blueberries and paper airplanes, you know what I mean?"
—Chad Johnson on JoJo Fletcher's season

The
BACHELOR
Bingo

THIS BINGO CARD IS GOOD FOR THE FANTASY SUITES EPISODE.

SOMEONE SAYS "COMMITMENT"	SOMEONE TALKS ABOUT THEIR HOMETOWN	THE BACHELOR SAYS, "CAN I WALK YOU OUT?"	THE HOST AND THE BACHELOR HAVE A SIT-DOWN	SOMEONE MENTIONS A BROTHER OR SISTER
THE BACHELOR SAYS SOMEONE WOULD BE A "GREAT WIFE"	SOMEONE IS SHOWN WEARING A ROBE	A WOMAN WALKS, LOOKING PENSIVE	THE COUPLE IS IN A HOT TUB	SOMEONE SAYS THEY ARE "SCARED"
THE COUPLE EATS BREAKFAST IN BED	THE FIRST WOMAN APPEARS AT THE ROSE CEREMONY	This free space is here for the right reasons.	SOMEONE SAYS THEY WANT CHILDREN	SOMEONE SAYS GOODBYE FROM A HOTEL BALCONY
SOMEONE MENTIONS GETTING ENGAGED AT THE END	SOMEONE SAYS THEY'RE "IN LOVE"	SOMEONE SAYS THEY CAN DO THEIR JOB "ANYWHERE"	SOMEONE MAKES THE BACHELOR LAUGH	SOMEONE TALKS ABOUT WANTING TO "BUILD A LIFE"
SOMEONE SAYS THE BACHELOR WOULD BE A GREAT DAD	SOMEONE MENTIONS THEIR CAREER	SOMEONE SAYS THE WORD "BUTTERFLIES"	SOMEONE SAYS THEY ARE "CONFIDENT"	THE BACHELOR ENTERS A HOTEL ROOM WITH SOMEONE

FUN FACT: Production teams change the interior of the Bachelor Mansion each season.

CUT ON DOTTED LINE TO USE THIS BINGO BOARD!

The
BACHELOR
Bingo

SOMEONE SAYS THE WORD "JOURNEY"	THE BACHELOR LOOKS AT ENGAGEMENT RINGS	A WOMAN PUTS ON MAKEUP	SOMEONE JUMPS INTO THE BACHELOR'S ARMS	SOMEBODY WRITES IN A JOURNAL
SOMEONE LOOKS SHOCKED IN THE LIVE AUDIENCE	THE BACHELOR SAYS HE KNOWS WHO HIS FINAL CHOICE IS	THE BACHELOR SAYS "BUT" TO THE WOMAN NOT CHOSEN	THE HOST FIRST APPEARS	A PEAR-SHAPED DIAMOND IS SHOWN
THE BACHELOR GETS DOWN ON ONE KNEE	SOMEONE IS BLEEPED FOR PROFANITY	This free space is on an amazing journey	THE BACHELOR TELLS HIS FAMILY ABOUT THE WOMEN	HOST SAYS "FIRST TIME IN BACHELOR HISTORY"
SOMEONE GIVES THE BACHELOR A GIFT	THE BACHELOR PICKS UP FINAL CHOICE AND SWINGS HER AROUND	THE BACHELOR HAS A ONE-ON-ONE WITH A PARENT	THE BACHELOR SAYS HE'S IN LOVE WITH BOTH WOMEN	SOMEONE SAYS THE WORD "PROCESS"
A HANDMADE SIGN IS SHOWN IN THE LIVE AUDIENCE	SOMEONE SAYS THE WORD "AMAZING"	A BIRD IS SHOWN FLYING	THE BACHELOR CRIES OVER HIS IMPENDING DECISION	THE BACHELOR OFFERS THE FINAL ROSE

FUN FACT: The Bachelor Mansion is massive at more than 10,000 square feet.

CUT ON DOTTED LINE TO USE THIS BINGO BOARD!

The
BACHELOR
Bingo

THIS BINGO CARD IS GOOD FOR "THE BACHELOR" FINALE.

CUT ON DOTTED LINE TO USE THIS BINGO BOARD!

THE BACHELOR SAYS HE IS IN LOVE WITH TWO PEOPLE	SHOES ARE SHOWN GETTING OUT OF LIMO	HOST REFERS TO SHOW ENDING AS "DRAMATIC"	SOMEONE LOOKS SHOCKED IN THE LIVE AUDIENCE	SOMEONE SAYS "EMERALD CUT"
A HANDMADE SIGN IS SHOWN IN THE LIVE AUDIENCE	THE BACHELOR GETS DOWN ON ONE KNEE	A PEAR-SHAPED DIAMOND IS SHOWN	THE BACHELOR SAYS HE KNOWS WHO HIS FINAL CHOICE IS	A WOMAN WEARS A WHITE DRESS TO THE FINAL CEREMONY
SOMEONE MENTIONS WANTING MARRIAGE	OVERHEAD SHOT OF FINAL ROSE CEREMONY AREA	This free space is on an amazing journey	NEXT BACHELORETTE IS ANNOUNCED	THE BACHELOR OFFERS THE FINAL ROSE
THE BACHELOR SAYS HE'S IN LOVE WITH BOTH WOMEN	SOMEONE SAYS THE WORD "AMAZING"	SOMEONE ACTUALLY TAKES A BITE OF FOOD	THE HOST WELCOMES THE FIRST WOMAN TO THE FINAL CEREMONY	THE REJECTED BACHELORETTE DRIVES AWAY
THE BACHELOR SAYS "BUT" TO THE WOMAN NOT CHOSEN	SOMEONE DABS THEIR EYES WITH A TISSUE	SOMEBODY WRITES IN A JOURNAL	THE BACHELOR PICKS UP FINAL CHOICE AND SWINGS HER AROUND	A WOMAN PUTS ON MAKEUP

QUOTABLE: "Is it awkward if I ask you for a better kiss?"
—Lace Morris on Ben Higgin's season

The BACHELOR *Bingo*

THIS BINGO CARD IS GOOD FOR "THE BACHELOR" FINALE.

CUT ON DOTTED LINE TO USE THIS BINGO BOARD!

THE BACHELOR PRETEND-THREATENS TO QUIT	THE BACHELOR TELLS HIS FAMILY ABOUT THE WOMEN	HOST REMINDS BACHELOR THAT "HE'S IN CHARGE"	THE BACHELOR HOLDS HANDS WITH SOMEONE	HOST SAYS "FIRST TIME IN BACHELOR HISTORY"
SOMEONE SAYS THE WORD "JOURNEY"	THE BACHELOR SAYS HE'S IN LOVE WITH BOTH WOMEN	A HANDMADE SIGN IS SHOWN IN THE LIVE AUDIENCE	A BIRD IS SHOWN FLYING	SOMEONE IS BLEEPED FOR PROFANITY
THE BACHELOR CLINKS GLASSES WITH SOMEONE	THE REJECTED BACHELORETTE DRIVES AWAY	This free space is on an amazing journey	THE BACHELOR GETS DOWN ON ONE KNEE	THE BACHELOR LOOKS AT ENGAGEMENT RINGS
NEXT BACHELORETTE IS ANNOUNCED	SOMEONE SAYS "EMERALD CUT"	THE BACHELOR SAYS HE IS IN LOVE WITH TWO PEOPLE	SOMEONE MENTIONS THEIR PARENTS' MARRIAGE	THE BACHELOR SAYS "BUT" TO THE WOMAN NOT CHOSEN
SOMEONE TALKS ABOUT WANTING CHILDREN	THE BACHELOR SAYS HE KNOWS WHO HIS FINAL CHOICE IS	SOMEONE LOOKS SHOCKED IN THE LIVE AUDIENCE	SOMEONE TOUCHES THE BACHELOR'S LEG	THE BACHELOR HAS A ONE-ON-ONE WITH A PARENT

FUN FACT: Season 16 winner Courtney Robertson wrote a book called "I Didn't Come Here to Make Friends."

The BACHELOR Bingo

THIS BINGO CARD IS GOOD FOR "THE BACHELOR" FINALE.

CUT ON DOTTED LINE TO USE THIS BINGO BOARD!

A PEAR-SHAPED DIAMOND IS SHOWN	THE BACHELOR HAS A ONE-ON-ONE WITH A PARENT	THE BACHELOR PICKS UP FINAL CHOICE AND SWINGS HER AROUND	SOMEONE SAYS THE WORD "WEDDING"	A WOMAN IS SHOWN TAKING A DEEP BREATH
SOMEBODY WRITES IN A JOURNAL	THE BACHELOR HOLDS HANDS WITH SOMEONE	SOMEONE TOUCHES THE BACHELOR'S LEG	THE BACHELOR STROLLS, LOOKING PENSIVE	THE BACHELOR CRIES OVER HIS IMPENDING DECISION
A WOMAN WEARS A WHITE DRESS TO THE FINAL CEREMONY	SOMEONE LOOKS SHOCKED IN THE LIVE AUDIENCE	This free space is on an amazing journey	SHOES ARE SHOWN GETTING OUT OF LIMO	SOMEONE SAYS THE WORD "CONNECTION"
OVERHEAD SHOT OF FINAL ROSE CEREMONY AREA	A WOMAN PUTS ON MAKEUP	THE BACHELOR GETS DOWN ON ONE KNEE	SOMEONE SAYS, "I SAID I WOULDN'T CRY"	THE HOST FIRST APPEARS
THE HOST WELCOMES THE FIRST WOMAN TO THE FINAL CEREMONY	SOMEONE IS BLEEPED FOR PROFANITY	HOST REFERS TO SHOW ENDING AS "DRAMATIC"	THE BACHELOR IS REUNITED WITH HIS FINAL CHOICE	NEXT BACHELORETTE IS ANNOUNCED

FUN FACT: If a couple calls off their engagement before two years, they have to return the ring.

The BACHELOR Bingo

THIS BINGO CARD IS GOOD FOR "THE BACHELOR" FINALE.

SOMEONE LOOKS SHOCKED IN THE LIVE AUDIENCE	THE BACHELOR GETS DOWN ON ONE KNEE	THE BACHELOR IS SHOWN SHOWERING	SOMEONE SAYS "MY PERSON"	THE BACHELOR SAYS HE IS IN LOVE WITH TWO PEOPLE
THE REJECTED BACHELORETTE DRIVES AWAY	SOMEONE SAYS THAT "FAMILY IS IMPORTANT"	THE BACHELOR LOOKS AT ENGAGEMENT RINGS	THE BACHELOR OFFERS THE FINAL ROSE	BACHELOR QUESTIONS IF SOMEONE IS "READY" FOR MARRIAGE
SOMEONE SAYS THE WORD "CONNECTION"	A HANDMADE SIGN IS SHOWN IN THE LIVE AUDIENCE	This free space is on an amazing journey	NEXT BACHELORETTE IS ANNOUNCED	THE BACHELOR PRETEND-THREATENS TO QUIT
A BIRD IS SHOWN FLYING	SOMEONE TALKS ABOUT THEIR PARENTS' DIVORCE	SOMEONE SAYS "EMERALD CUT"	SOMEBODY WRITES IN A JOURNAL	THE BACHELOR TELLS HIS FAMILY ABOUT THE WOMEN
THE BACHELOR SAYS HE KNOWS WHO HIS FINAL CHOICE IS	THE BACHELOR PICKS UP FINAL CHOICE AND SWINGS HER AROUND	THE BACHELOR'S PARENT SAYS WHICH WOMAN IS BEST CHOICE	SOMEONE IS VISIBLY SWEATING	SOMEONE SAYS THE WORD "SPECIAL"

FUN FACT: "The Bachelorette" has a higher success rate than "The Bachelor."

CUT ON DOTTED LINE TO USE THIS BINGO BOARD!

The BACHELOR *Bingo*

A WOMAN WEARS A WHITE DRESS TO THE FINAL CEREMONY	THE BACHELOR IS REUNITED WITH HIS FINAL CHOICE	A HANDMADE SIGN IS SHOWN IN THE LIVE AUDIENCE	THE BACHELOR SAYS "BUT" TO THE WOMAN NOT CHOSEN	OVERHEAD SHOT OF FINAL ROSE CEREMONY AREA
NEXT BACHELORETTE IS ANNOUNCED	THE BACHELOR CRIES OVER HIS IMPENDING DECISION	FORMER BACHELOR SHOWN IN LIVE AUDIENCE	SHOES ARE SHOWN GETTING OUT OF LIMO	A PEAR-SHAPED DIAMOND IS SHOWN
THE HOST WELCOMES THE FIRST WOMAN TO THE FINAL CEREMONY	HOST SAYS "FIRST TIME IN BACHELOR HISTORY"	This free space is on an amazing journey	THE BACHELOR IS SHOWN SHOWERING	THE BACHELOR GETS DOWN ON ONE KNEE
THE BACHELOR'S PARENT SAYS WHICH WOMAN IS BEST CHOICE	THE BACHELOR HAS A ONE-ON-ONE WITH A PARENT	SOMEONE IS BLEEPED FOR PROFANITY	THE BACHELOR LOOKS AT ENGAGEMENT RINGS	A WOMAN PUTS ON MAKEUP
SOMEONE SAYS THEY WANT CHILDREN	A WOMAN IS SHOWN TAKING A DEEP BREATH	SOMEONE SAYS "COMMITMENT"	SOMEONE SAYS THEY ARE "SCARED"	SOMEONE SAYS "MY PERSON"

FUN FACT: Contestants can't use their cell phones, or regularly watch TV or read books.

CUT ON DOTTED LINE TO USE THIS BINGO BOARD!

The BACHELOR *Bingo*

FORMER BACHELOR SHOWN IN LIVE AUDIENCE	SOMEONE SAYS "EMERALD CUT"	THE BACHELOR SAYS HE IS IN LOVE WITH TWO PEOPLE	THE HOST APPEARS	THE BACHELOR SAYS HE KNOWS WHO HIS FINAL CHOICE IS
THE BACHELOR SAYS HE IS NERVOUS	THE BACHELOR GETS DOWN ON ONE KNEE	SOMEONE SAYS THE WORD "EXCITED"	A WOMAN WEARS A WHITE DRESS TO THE FINAL CEREMONY	THE BACHELOR IS SHOWN SHOWERING
SHOES ARE SHOWN GETTING OUT OF LIMO	THE BACHELOR TELLS HIS FAMILY ABOUT THE WOMEN	This free space is on an amazing journey	THE REJECTED BACHELORETTE DRIVES AWAY	HOST SAYS "FIRST TIME IN BACHELOR HISTORY"
THE BACHELOR SAYS "BUT" TO THE WOMAN NOT CHOSEN	THE BACHELOR PICKS UP FINAL CHOICE AND SWINGS HER AROUND	NEXT BACHELORETTE IS ANNOUNCED	HOST REFERS TO SHOW ENDING AS "DRAMATIC"	THE BACHELOR'S PARENT SAYS WHICH WOMAN IS BEST CHOICE
SOMEBODY WRITES IN A JOURNAL	THE BACHELOR PRETEND-THREATENS TO QUIT	A BIRD IS SHOWN FLYING	SOMEONE IS BLEEPED FOR PROFANITY	THE BACHELOR HAS A ONE-ON-ONE WITH A PARENT

FUN FACT: Cast members have to be at least 21 years old.

CUT ON DOTTED LINE TO USE THIS BINGO BOARD!

The BACHELOR *Bingo*

THE BACHELOR IS SHOWN SHOWERING	A WOMAN IS SHOWN TAKING A DEEP BREATH	THE BACHELOR SAYS HE'S IN LOVE WITH BOTH WOMEN	THE HOST AND THE BACHELOR HAVE A SIT-DOWN	THE BACHELOR GETS DOWN ON ONE KNEE
A WOMAN PUTS ON MAKEUP	HOST REFERS TO SHOW ENDING AS "DRAMATIC"	THE BACHELOR PRETEND-THREATENS TO QUIT	FORMER BACHELOR SHOWN IN LIVE AUDIENCE	SOMEONE SAYS THEY ARE "SCARED"
HOST SAYS "FIRST TIME IN BACHELOR HISTORY"	THE BACHELOR OFFERS THE FINAL ROSE	This free space is on an amazing journey	THE BACHELOR SAYS "BUT" TO THE WOMAN NOT CHOSEN	SOMEBODY WRITES IN A JOURNAL
OVERHEAD SHOT OF FINAL ROSE CEREMONY AREA	A HANDMADE SIGN IS SHOWN IN THE LIVE AUDIENCE	THE BACHELOR'S PARENT SAYS WHICH WOMAN IS BEST CHOICE	THE BACHELOR SAYS HE IS IN LOVE WITH TWO PEOPLE	SHOES ARE SHOWN GETTING OUT OF LIMO
THE BACHELOR LOOKS AT ENGAGEMENT RINGS	NEXT BACHELORETTE IS ANNOUNCED	SOMEONE SAYS THE WORD "BUTTERFLIES"	SOMEONE SAYS THEY ARE "CONFIDENT"	THE BACHELOR TELLS HIS FAMILY ABOUT THE WOMEN

FUN FACT: The Guinness Book of World Records site still lists Carly Waddell and Evan Bass as the record holders for the longest, hottest kiss.

CUT ON DOTTED LINE TO USE THIS BINGO BOARD!

BACHELOR
in paradise

THIS BINGO CARD IS GOOD FOR ANY "BACHELOR IN PARADISE" EPISODE.

CUT ON DOTTED LINE TO USE THIS BINGO BOARD!

MEN HAND OUT THE ROSES	TWO PEOPLE KISS IN THE POOL	SOMEONE WALKS ON THE BEACH	SOMEONE WEARS A WHITE BIKINI	A SEAGULL IS SHOWN
TINY UMBRELLA SHOWN IN DRINK	SOMEONE IS ACCUSED OF FORMING A RELATIONSHIP BEFOREHAND	SOMEONE SAYS "MEXICO"	A NEW PERSON ARRIVES ON BEACH	SOMEONE SAYS THEY ARE"OLD"
A ONE-ON-ONE DATE INVOLVES A CULTURAL CEREMONY	SOMEONE SAYS THEY WANT TO GET ENGAGED	This free space is knockin' on heaven's door.	SOMEONE ROLLS A SUITCASE	FUNNY TITLE SHOWS ON SCREEN DURING INDIVIDUAL INTERVIEW
SOMEONE MENTIONS A COUPLE WHO MARRIED ON THE SHOW	SOMEONE LISTS ALL COUPLES THAT HAVE FORMED SO FAR	BACHELOR CASTING COMMERCIAL SHOWN	A COUPLE STROLLS DOWN A STREET IN MEXICO ON A DATE	SOMEONE KISSES ON BEACH BED
SOMEONE LAYS IN HAMMOCK	SOMEONE WANTS TO GO "CHAT"	VOLLEYBALL NET OVER POOL IS SHOWN	WELLS MAKES A DRINK	SOMEONE QUITS THE SHOW

FUN FACT: The original "Bachelor in Paradise" bartender, Jorge, now owns a tour company in Mexico.

BACHELOR
in paradise

THIS BINGO CARD IS GOOD FOR ANY "BACHELOR IN PARADISE" EPISODE.

CUT ON DOTTED LINE TO USE THIS BINGO BOARD!

VOLLEYBALL NET OVER POOL IS SHOWN	CONVERSATION TAKES PLACE IN HOT TUB	SOMEONE CLIMBS ON BEACH BED	SOMEONE SITS WITH FEET IN POOL	DATE CARD ARRIVES
SOMEONE SAYS "MEXICO"	SOMEONE SAYS A COUPLE IS "SOLID"	SOMEONE CRIES	SOMEONE ROLLS THEIR EYES	WELLS MAKES A DRINK
SOMEONE WEARS A WHITE BIKINI	A SEAGULL IS SHOWN	This free space is knockin' on heaven's door.	MEN HAND OUT THE ROSES	SOMEONE LISTS ALL COUPLES THAT HAVE FORMED SO FAR
BACHELOR CASTING COMMERCIAL SHOWN	FUNNY TITLE SHOWS ON SCREEN DURING INDIVIDUAL INTERVIEW	A BODY PART IS CENSORED	SOMEONE IS "HOPING" FOR A SPECIFIC PERSON TO BE THERE	PERSON KISSES TWO OR MORE PEOPLE IN ONE DAY
FOUR OR MORE PEOPLE LAYING ON ONE BED	SOMEONE MENTIONS A BACHELOR NATION EX	SUNSET IS SHOWN	SOMEONE WANTS TO GO "CHAT"	TINY UMBRELLA SHOWN IN DRINK

FUN FACT: You can book a trip to the resort where they film "Bachelor in Paradise."

BACHELOR *in paradise*

THIS BINGO CARD IS GOOD FOR ANY "BACHELOR IN PARADISE" EPISODE.

CUT ON DOTTED LINE TO USE THIS BINGO BOARD!

SOMEONE KISSES ON BEACH BED	SOMEONE QUITS THE SHOW	SOMEONE SAYS THEY ARE "OLD"	SOMEONE SAYS "MEXICO"	CONVERSATION TAKES PLACE IN HOT TUB
SOMEONE SITS WITH FEET IN POOL	A COUPLE STROLLS DOWN A STREET IN MEXICO ON A DATE	A ONE-ON-ONE DATE INVOLVES A CULTURAL CEREMONY	TWO PEOPLE KISS IN THE POOL	SOMEONE SAYS THEY WANT TO GET ENGAGED
SOMEONE IS "HOPING" FOR A SPECIFIC PERSON TO BE THERE	TINY UMBRELLA SHOWN IN DRINK	This free space is knockin' on heaven's door.	SOMEONE IS ACCUSED OF FORMING A RELATIONSHIP BEFOREHAND	SOMEONE MENTIONS A COUPLE WHO MARRIED ON THE SHOW
SOMEONE WANTS TO GO "CHAT"	SOMEONE WALKS ON THE BEACH	SOMEONE ROLLS A SUITCASE	SOMEONE WEARS A WHITE BIKINI	A CRAB SCUTTLES BY
NEW PERSON ARRIVES, NO ONE KNOWS WHO IT IS	FOUR OR MORE PEOPLE LAYING ON ONE BED	MEN HAND OUT THE ROSES	SOMEONE LAYS IN HAMMOCK	SOMEONE LISTS ALL COUPLES THAT HAVE FORMED SO FAR

FUN FACT: The rooms on "Bachelor in Paradise" don't have air conditioning so that the contestants will be more likely to go out and mingle.

BACHELOR *in paradise*

THIS BINGO CARD IS GOOD FOR ANY "BACHELOR IN PARADISE" EPISODE.

CUT ON DOTTED LINE TO USE THIS BINGO BOARD!

DATE CARD ARRIVES	SOMEONE ROLLS THEIR EYES	SOMEONE CRIES	LOVE TRIANGLE FORMS	FUNNY TITLE SHOWS ON SCREEN DURING INDIVIDUAL INTERVIEW
SOMEONE MENTIONS A COUPLE WHO MARRIED ON THE SHOW	A NEW PERSON ARRIVES ON BEACH	A COUPLE STROLLS DOWN A STREET IN MEXICO ON A DATE	SOMEONE MENTIONS A BACHELOR NATION EX	WOMEN HAND OUT THE ROSES
CONVERSATION TAKES PLACE IN HOT TUB	A CRAB SCUTTLES BY	This free space is knockin' on heaven's door.	BACHELOR CASTING COMMERCIAL SHOWN	SOMEONE CLIMBS ON BEACH BED
SOMEONE LISTS ALL COUPLES THAT HAVE FORMED SO FAR	SOMEONE WEARS A WHITE BIKINI	SOMEONE QUITS THE SHOW	SOMEONE SAYS THEY ARE "OLD"	A BODY PART IS CENSORED
MEN HAND OUT THE ROSES	SOMEONE ROLLS A SUITCASE	PERSON KISSES TWO OR MORE PEOPLE IN ONE DAY	SOMEONE SAYS "MEXICO"	VOLLEYBALL NET OVER POOL IS SHOWN

FUN FACT: Men wear necklaces on "Bachelor in Paradise" to hold their microphones.

BACHELOR *in paradise*

THIS BINGO CARD IS GOOD FOR ANY "BACHELOR IN PARADISE" EPISODE.

WELLS MAKES A DRINK	SOMEONE WEARS A SARONG	A SEAGULL IS SHOWN	WOMEN HAND OUT THE ROSES	A ONE-ON-ONE DATE INVOLVES A CULTURAL CEREMONY
SOMEONE IS ACCUSED OF FORMING A RELATIONSHIP BEFOREHAND	LOVE TRIANGLE FORMS	A ONE-ON-ONE DATE INVOLVES MUD AND/OR MASSAGE	SOMEONE KISSES ON BEACH BED	SOMEONE WALKS ON THE BEACH
SOMEONE HAS A DRINK IN A COCONUT	TWO PEOPLE KISS IN THE POOL	*This free space is knockin' on heaven's door.*	FOUR OR MORE PEOPLE LAYING ON ONE BED	SOMEONE SAYS A COUPLE IS "SOLID"
SOMEONE ROLLS THEIR EYES	SOMEONE LAYS IN HAMMOCK	NEW PERSON ARRIVES, NO ONE KNOWS WHO IT IS	TINY UMBRELLA SHOWN IN DRINK	SOMEONE IS "HOPING" FOR A SPECIFIC PERSON TO BE THERE
SOMEONE SAYS THEY WANT TO GET ENGAGED	SOMEONE MENTIONS A COUPLE WHO MARRIED ON THE SHOW	A BODY PART IS CENSORED	PERSON KISSES TWO OR MORE PEOPLE IN ONE DAY	SOMEONE WANTS TO GO "CHAT"

FUN FACT: Marcus Grodd and Lacy Faddoul were the first couple to get engaged on "Bachelor in Paradise."

CUT ON DOTTED LINE TO USE THIS BINGO BOARD!

BACHELOR *in paradise*

THIS BINGO CARD IS GOOD FOR ANY "BACHELOR IN PARADISE" EPISODE.

A ONE-ON-ONE DATE INVOLVES MUD AND/OR MASSAGE	SOMEONE WANTS TO GO "CHAT"	FOUR OR MORE PEOPLE LAYING ON ONE BED	WELLS MAKES A DRINK	SOMEONE SITS WITH FEET IN POOL
FUNNY TITLE SHOWS ON SCREEN DURING INDIVIDUAL INTERVIEW	BACHELOR CASTING COMMERCIAL SHOWN	SOMEONE MENTIONS A COUPLE WHO MARRIED ON THE SHOW	LOVE TRIANGLE FORMS	SOMEONE HAS A DRINK IN A COCONUT
SOMEONE CLIMBS ON BEACH BED	WOMEN HAND OUT THE ROSES	This free space is knockin' on heaven's door.	A COUPLE STROLLS DOWN A STREET IN MEXICO ON A DATE	DATE CARD ARRIVES
SOMEONE SAYS THEY ARE "OLD"	SOMEONE MENTIONS A BACHELOR NATION EX	SOMEONE LISTS ALL COUPLES THAT HAVE FORMED SO FAR	SOMEONE WEARS A SARONG	SOMEONE ROLLS A SUITCASE
A SEAGULL IS SHOWN	VOLLEYBALL NET OVER POOL IS SHOWN	TWO PEOPLE KISS IN THE POOL	SOMEONE SAYS A COUPLE IS "SOLID"	A NEW PERSON ARRIVES ON BEACH

FUN FACT: The are 22 children born to parents who met in Bachelor Nation – and counting!

BACHELOR *in paradise*

SOMEONE WEARS A SARONG	SOMEONE IS "HOPING" FOR A SPECIFIC PERSON TO BE THERE	SOMEONE LAYS IN HAMMOCK	CONVERSATION TAKES PLACE IN HOT TUB	A CRAB SCUTTLES BY
SOMEONE CRIES	TINY UMBRELLA SHOWN IN DRINK	SOMEONE WALKS ON THE BEACH	A ONE-ON-ONE DATE INVOLVES MUD AND/OR MASSAGE	NEW PERSON ARRIVES, NO ONE KNOWS WHO IT IS
SOMEONE ROLLS A SUITCASE	WELLS MAKES A DRINK	This free space is knockin' on heaven's door.	SOMEONE IS ACCUSED OF FORMING A RELATIONSHIP BEFOREHAND	SOMEONE SAYS THEY WANT TO GET ENGAGED
A BODY PART IS CENSORED	A ONE-ON-ONE DATE INVOLVES A CULTURAL CEREMONY	LOVE TRIANGLE FORMS	SOMEONE KISSES ON BEACH BED	SOMEONE SAYS THEY ARE "OLD"
WOMEN HAND OUT THE ROSES	SOMEONE SAYS A COUPLE IS "SOLID"	SOMEONE SITS WITH FEET IN POOL	SOMEONE ROLLS THEIR EYES	FUNNY TITLE SHOWS ON SCREEN DURING INDIVIDUAL INTERVIEW

FUN FACT: The average Bachelor relationship lasts three months and 16 days after the season finale airs.

CUT ON DOTTED LINE TO USE THIS BINGO BOARD!

BACHELOR *in paradise*

THIS BINGO CARD IS GOOD FOR ANY "BACHELOR IN PARADISE" EPISODE.

A BODY PART IS CENSORED	SOMEONE ROLLS THEIR EYES	SOMEONE IS "HOPING" FOR A SPECIFIC PERSON TO BE THERE	SOMEONE MENTIONS A BACHELOR NATION EX	A ONE-ON-ONE DATE INVOLVES A CULTURAL CEREMONY
SOMEONE SAYS A COUPLE IS "SOLID"	TWO PEOPLE KISS IN THE POOL	SOMEONE CRIES	SOMEONE MENTIONS A COUPLE WHO MARRIED ON THE SHOW	A ONE-ON-ONE DATE INVOLVES MUD AND/OR MASSAGE
NEW PERSON ARRIVES, NO ONE KNOWS WHO IT IS	SOMEONE SITS WITH FEET IN POOL	This free space is knockin' on heaven's door.	SOMEONE CLIMBS ON BEACH BED	WELLS MAKES A DRINK
FUNNY TITLE SHOWS ON SCREEN DURING INDIVIDUAL INTERVIEW	SOMEONE HAS A DRINK IN A COCONUT	CONVERSATION TAKES PLACE IN HOT TUB	SOMEONE WEARS A SARONG	VOLLEYBALL NET OVER POOL IS SHOWN
DATE CARD ARRIVES	WOMEN HAND OUT THE ROSES	A CRAB SCUTTLES BY	LOVE TRIANGLE FORMS	SOMEONE QUITS THE SHOW

FUN FACT: The average age of contestants on "The Bachelor" is 26.

CUT ON DOTTED LINE TO USE THIS BINGO BOARD!

LIMO ARRIVAL TRUE OR FALSE GAME

BONUS GAME!

To play, simply cut out the cards below and place them face down in a stack. Take turns reading and answering the true/false questions. One point is earned for each correct answer. The player with the most points at the end wins! You can use this game during commercial breaks.

CUT ON DOTTED LINE TO USE THIS BINGO BOARD!

True or false: A contestant arrived on a forklift — TRUE! Tino Franco (Season: Gabby and Rachel)	True or false: A contestant gave the Bachelor an urn full of her ex's ashes — TRUE! Jill Chin (Season: Clayton Echard)	True or false: A contestant showed up with a blow-up doll — TRUE! Cody Menk (Season: Katie Thurston)
True or false: A contestant arrived in a sloth costume — TRUE! Alex Dillon (Season: Colton Underwood)	True or false: A contestant arrived wearing a prosthetic belly to look pregnant — TRUE! Clare Crawley (Season: Juan Pablo Galavis)	True or false: A contestant arrived dressed as Donald Trump — FALSE! Nobody tried to Make the Bachelor Great Again
True or false: A contestant arrived wearing a unicorn head — TRUE! Jojo Fletcher (Season: Ben Higgins)	True or false: A contestant arrived in a hot tub on a flatbed truck — FALSE! The last thing this show needs is more hot tubs	True or false: A contestant arrived as a giant paper airplane — TRUE! Madison Prewett (Season: Peter Weber)
True or false: A contestant arrived inside a suitcase — TRUE! Kiarra Norman (Season: Peter Weber)	True or false: A contestant rode in on a camel — TRUE! Lacey Mark (Season: Nick Viall)	True or false: A contestant arrived with her parents — FALSE! Although a contestant did have her grandmother arrive in her place once
True or false: A contestant arrived brushing her teeth — FALSE! But a contestant did spray the Bachelor's mouth with breath freshener	True or false: A contestant arrived in a coffin — FALSE! Never happened Although there's a good "dead on arrival" joke in here somewhere	True or false: A contestant arrived in a rose hat saying, "I AM the first impression rose" — TRUE! Mandi Kremer (Season: Ben Higgins)
True or false: A contestant arrived dressed as a windmill — TRUE! Deandra Kanu (Season: Peter Weber)	True or false: A contestant arrived riding a zebra — FALSE! Although several Bachelor entrances have involved animals	True or false: A contestant arrived and pulled out a 12-pack of condoms — TRUE! Kylie Ramos (Season: Peter Weber)
True or false: A contestant arrived via hang glider — FALSE! Although a contestant did arrive via helicopter	True or false: A contestant arrived in a wedding dress — TRUE! Lindsey Yenter (Season: Sean Lowe)	True or false: A contestant arrived in a shark costume — TRUE! Alexis Waters (Season: Nick Viall)

VILLAINS GOTTA VILL TRIVIA GAME

To play, simply cut out the cards below and place them face down in a stack. Take turns reading and answering the trivia questions. One point is earned for each correct answer. (A first name is enough to earn the points.) The player with the most points at the end wins! You can use this game during commercial breaks.

CUT ON DOTTED LINE TO USE THIS BINGO BOARD!

What Bachelor villain said she was bullied for having cankles? Olivia Caridi (Season: Ben Higgins)	**What Bachelor villain is known for eating too many shrimp?** Shanae Ankney (Season: Clayton Echard)	**What Bachelorette villain was called a "turd" by Amy Schumer?** JJ Lane (Season: Kaitlyn Bristowe)
What Bachelor villain said she couldn't control her eyebrows? Tierra LiCausi (Season: Sean Lowe)	**What villain was sent packing after calling the Bachelorette "shallow"?** Ian Tomson (Season: Kaitlyn Bristowe)	**What Bachelor winner had a reputation as a spoiled daddy's girl?** Vienna Girardi (Season: Jake Pavelka)
What villain left the show after having an affair with a producer? Rozlyn Papa (Season: Jake Pavelka)	**What Bachelor villain wore a shirt that said "Gold Digger"?** Trish Schneider (Season: Jesse Palmer)	**What villain referred to the Bachelorette's child as "baggage"?** Kalon McMahon (Season: Emily Maynard)
What Bachelor villain spoke often of her late husband? Kelsey Poe (Season: Chris Soules)	**What Bachelorette winner was later revealed to have a girlfriend back home?** Jed Wyatt (Season: Hannah Brown)	**What Bachelor villain sprayed whipped cream on her cleavage?** Corinne Olympios (Season: Nick Viall)
What Bachelorette villain bragged about making Final Four with a girlfriend? Wes Hayden (Season: Jillian Harris)	**What Bachelor villain was known for saying, "Winning!"?** Courtney Robertson (Season: Ben Flajnik)	**What Bachelor *and* villain is known for saying, "It's OK"?** Juan Pablo Galavis (Season: Juan Pablo Galavis)
What villain called the Bachelorette an "ugly duckling"? Bentley Williams (Season: Ashley Hebert)	**What Bachelorette villain talked constantly about his religion?** Luke Parker (Season: Hannah Brown)	**What Bachelorette villain wore gold hot pants?** Jordan Kimball (Season: Becca Kufrin)
What Bachelorette villain threatened to "cut off someone's torso"? Chad Johnson (Season: JoJo Fletcher)	**What Bachelor villain used a fake baby voice?** Krystal Nielsen (Season: Arie Luyendyk)]	**What Bachelor villain wore a tiara and said she was a queen?** Victoria Larson (Season: Matt James)

Made in the USA
Columbia, SC
06 December 2024

48549729R00059